Ralph Hawkins

Also by Ralph Hawkins:

English Literature, The Many Press, London, 1979
Well, You Could Do, Curiously Strong, London, 1979
The Word from the One, Galloping Dog Press,
                                        Newcastle-upon-Tyne, 1980
Soft in the Brains, Spanner, London, 1981
Tell Me No More And Tell Me, Grosseteste, Leeds & Wirksworth, 1981
Birds, Cattle, Fish & Flies, Lamb, London, 1981
At Last Away, Galloping Dog Press, Newcastle-upon-Tyne, 1988
Within & Without, Silver Hounds, Laughton, 1992
Writ, Active in Airtime, Colchester, 1993
Routes & Abrasions, Poetical Histories, Cambridge, 1993
Flecks, Oasis Books & Permanent Press, London, 1995
Pelt, Active in Airtime, Brightlingsea, 1998
Part One Puškin, Poetical Histories, Cambridge, 1998
The Coiling Dragon / The Scarlet Bird / The White Tiger / A Blue & Misted Shroud,
                                        Equipage, Cambridge, 2000
Pool, Writers Forum, London, 2000
The Primeval Atom, Writers Forum, London, 2000

(with Bob Cobbing)
G Curled Ribbon, Writers Forum, London, 2000
a split, Writers Forum, London, 2000
A Quonk, Writers Forum, London, 2001
Signatures or the Wasp Under Custard, Writers Forum, London, 2001
Gloria, Writers Forum, London, 2001
The Next Morning, Writers Forum, London, 2002
Everyday Pursuits, Writers Forum, London, 2002

The MOON, The Chief Hairdresser (highlights)

Ralph Hawkins

First published in 2004 in the United Kingdom by

Shearsman Books
58 Velwell Road
Exeter EX4 4LD

http://www.shearsman.com/

ISBN 0-907562-42-6

Copyright © Ralph Hawkins, 2002, 2003, 2004.
All rights reserved. The right of Ralph Hawkins to be identified as the author of this work has been asserted by him in accordance with the Copyrights, Designs and Patents Act of 1988. All rights reserved. No part of this publication may be reproduced, stored in a retrieval system, transmitted in any form or by any means, electronic, mechanical, photocopying, recording or otherwise, without the prior permission of the publisher.

Rear cover photograph of the author by Jean Hawkins. Copyright © Jean Hawkins, 2004.

Some of these poems have previously appeared in *Oasis, The North, Shearsman, The Gig, The Alterran Poetry Assemblage* and *April Eye – Poems for Peter Riley*. *Part One Puškin* originally appeared as a pamphlet from Poetical Histories.

This book is for

Bob Cobbing 1920-2002
and
Douglas Oliver 1937-2000

CONTENTS

The MOON, The Chief Hairdresser (highlights)

The Sylph in Stockings	11
The Secret of the Sylph	12
The Sylph in Tights	13
The Sylph and the Barbecue	14
Rooms	15
Poem (*I have in mind here one of Brancusi's birds*)	20
Some Signs	22
Poesia	23
Poem 25B	25
Poem (*We need a better understanding...*)	27
Poem (*Before I begin this poem*)	29
Poem 2 (*today it is snowing in Naples*)	30
The Leisure Industry	31
The Pictures	33
Paris	40
Find the Black Sea	43
Homer in Paris	45
Catskill on a locomotive	46
capital worries (the clean out)	47
in the pipeline, see below	48
An Interlude	49
One's Confusion With The East	50
A History of Hydraulics	51
First Anti Poem	52
XXXXXXXXXXXXXXXX	54
The Next Poem	55
The Artist's Life	57
This poem is concerned with...	58
This Poem	59
1. The poet intended to write a poem of a tree	60
Temptress: A Timeless Theme	61
Temptress Two	63
Temptress Thee	64
Temptress Three	65
Tempted	66
Tosso the Great	68

Part One Puškin   75

Puškin Part Two   85

The Littoral Zone   95

Uruk   103

The MOON,
The Chief Hairdresser
(highlights)

The Sylph in Stockings

Airy or Shadowy Ones
are baffled by phylacteries of dog's droppings
and a snake's head
is sovereign against baleful manifestations

Never wander off humming
with a notion to bathe in lonely mountain pools
WARNING water-girls hang out there

Carry dog-lites in your pocket
to shame their nakedness
their rich sticky-bud honey-stuck nipples

Don't get half arsed strolling at night

Don't stop for a piss behind a tree
gazing up at Orion's Belt
because old goat-man will stop by

Carry some sliced tortoise meat as a counter-spell
keep a prophylactic in your back pocket
or you may swell up and die

The Shadowy Ones will make friends with dogs
knowing the wolf-whistle by heart
they will learn your name and call it on the wind

They have no shame naked as daylight

They will sit around welcoming fires at night
playing their enticing flutes of random and chaos

The Secret of the Sylph

He opened the ice-box in which he was keeping
THE SECRET OF THE SYLPH
when his eye was distracted by a cold compote of plums
he made an ORION'S BELT of plum stones
and a garland of literary devices

the sylph always wore a device below her belt

Now if the night sky were hair
then the stars would be jewels
and the moon the chief hairdresser

the sky is a net holding the stars for fish to swim through

THE SECRET OF THE SYLPH
and closed the box

The Sylph in Tights

Trees are their dwelling places

garlands are plaited phylacteries

If you lop, chop or fell a tree enchant counter charms

thorn trees and the wild pear have repelling properties
as does the ripe honey flower

box is also a powerful apotropaic
one drop will make you taller than an oak

they will not be able to stop you
gatecrashing their wild parties

you will stride from one mountain to the next
you will never grow old

your favourite pastimes will be naked running
naked wrestling and naked horseback riding

The Sylph and the Barbecue

good and bad omens can be discerned in the fight of birds
(the Ostrich and the Emu)

study the leftover litter of barbecues
learn to haruspicate from entrails
the marinade of wild mountain thyme, red basil and virgin olive oil
the spread of chicken wings
the tossed tissue*

the beadless eye of the vulture one watching for moments of
        weakness and indiscretion

carry dog lites
droppings
nutmeg

it is very important to lay the lamb on a flattened branch before
        you cut its throat

DON'T LOOK INTO THE EYES

roast it whole on a spit

study its guts for mantic significance

ENJOY
Have a few beers

* I tried this at a home-brew party. There was lots of merrymaking and some mild transvestism

omens are shit

Rooms

Who is that with a bulb on his head?
The sentence for poetry is life not waffle.
Is not the string of unbroken rain more
Elegiac than pain or suffering?
And do we care of suffering
Putting up sound baffles, artificial disclaimers and orthography.
You may well scrape by with a 2H pencil
He could muster a coloured orb
(Here a hymnic aspect is apparent)
(I thought of whales, lantern fish and carbuncles).
How can bulb be bump and waffle food?

ii

The problem is to disconnect
(these things come to mind)
Whales have more blubber than poetry?
True or filched? Disjoining or [   ] erased.
Birds thread a spectrum on lard or birdy fat.
The river (ribbon) washes over in rhyme
its torrid tale full of fish
banded toothcarp and Evangeline's lyretail.
The idiosyncrasy of the brushstroke is
always contingent upon the ontological
(now there's a word full of beating)

iii

Beaming he has a bump on his writing
How can this bulb work?
Ting goes elasticity mapping androgyny in Chaucer
Making girdles for gowns in limited overs
Making out the deepest metacritiques of signification
Also contingent upon the ontological.
O how I must extend these lines until they float with syllables
Two's three's and five's (now that the omens have gone)
A bump is now a blimp & a POOM will enter my life

iv

there's a weak blimp blimp blimp on the transmission
there must be a bump on his writing as
she wipes off the milkiest of wheys cross-directional
arrows to and fromage on the map
pleonastically undercutting meaning
(there are limited temporal spans to tropes)
the prose of St Augustine
words so jammed together the flame doesn't spout
(disconnect from blubber)
move to grove or fields of thistle, throstle and the lark
cut in with jaunty flights forsaken
over where I'm punctuated
is not all I wish for of these aporias

v

use glue as a connector
everytime there's a smudge there's a blob on his writing
PVA St Augustine
in adapting thumb index to number I realise how disconnected I
blob and bump and blimp
consider the following examples,
a confluence, a torrid full of fish, a passional,
a hypertext to the transcendental
where writing spouts
hooked, glued by thumb and fin
sailing off
he has a wonderful corkscrew
tail (a picture). Do you think he is scary enough?
Now describe the other two figures
describe her flowing limbs (a Sylph)
describe her naked
describe the horse
blob blob blob

Poem

I have in mind here one of Brancusi's birds
(set the number of lines to sixteen
include some performance indicators,
some topical adjunct
have a focus or a subject, some Latin)

(Mrs Pink hanging out the washing
       sexual and economic matters
          hose and pants)

floating orthogonal lines creating
tension within and between words

the constant of what the written misses, evades,
between the straight and the curved

      (Betti's flat stomach
as Fumihiko below Fuji)

the sensual abandon of shaped space, of passages
(the footnote to line 10)
and points of juncture give the poem a sense
of fluidity and movement

these curves one senses
have left the realm of rational constructs.
Unusual spaces (between letters, words, lines, stanzas
And unexpected scenes

                    which lead us to

and **BLACK CYPRESSES**
with his hat on in her hat putting on her

gloves to go out in the red of Jephtha's dress
in front of a donkey do a third girl
at the feet of a girl who holds it

reduce me to tears wears a short dress
the thighs interlocking chalky
the hills covered with the undulations of armies
(Dec 2001) the readiness of a quiet town
spared by war spared from war
the immediate sound of guns
from Colchester firing range

Some Signs

I cannot be accused of being an innovator

I shall prepare a great poem
and my readers will gather in crowds

what words there are in the rain
Biddi and Betti doing the lottery,
a swimming pool, a caravan

Mrs Pink a holiday in the White House
re-do the garden

but I'm letting the poem slip

the forest echoed with voices
the night lit up with bright lights (almost deranged)
the saint stood before the crib and his heat overflowed

how old I am now
my wife and children

poems written in riddles
the efficacy of which is discussed in
closed circles

what is integrity

and the hay from the crib
was kept by the people
afterwards cured
sick animals
and drove off pestilence

Poesia

Giorgione came from Castelfranco, northwest of Venice
I have written to her two or three times
She ignores me
The third is artifice
The fourth *poesia*
                        my theory is that only the words
                        in composition move both in
                        literal and figurative combinations
                        the overall movement is lateral

Giorgione pushed three figures to the side, *La Tempestà*
I scour the pages
scroll the screen
what offence have I committed
softly spoken from the desert

I read somewhere Renoir's paintbrush was a penis
Which puts a lie to the words
A certain horizontality
"with this small painting visual poetry has been born"
and it may well be possible to read Venice as Venus
thereby setting up a depth of movement on a sonic level

her red lips, her creamy body lies
                        her left hand holding her genitals
here
alone
you may think who your friends are
and what do they mean

contrapposto
there is an *S* curve to the body
of sensuous skin

the stallion on the lid
the rabbits in the field

one reading of visual artifice is static
although the eye and mind wander

some people you like
others you disregard
I will write again, maybe, one day
to the trees and sky at night

Poem 25B

a *S*eraph came to rest in my ear

a line of sight
like a slight of hand
in a boat by Alfred Wallis

he had wings

and the embossed margins
eschewed the errors of
the nebulous centre

a ferry across the water

one line like a wave
runs into another
a patterning effect
abandoned before begun
unlike a narrative or
allegorical construction
where you might wish for
a corbelled arcade of leafy garlands
which only satisfy
linear and schematised forms
harbouring hidden intention

only this morning Jean produced
some small *wish-figures*
to place under my pillow

a *S*eraph came to my ear

he could be saddened and weep
he could close his eyes and offend
he could have mood-swings and tantrums
he could be jealous and
refuse his thaumaturigical activities

Poem

We need a better understanding of
the meaning of *effect* in poetry

One effect of the poems of John Ashbery
is penetrable loss
filled with weak shadows
a sunless, gently luminous day
when what we would
more demand is a defined
relief from our catalogue of woes

all is fog shimmer, haze, smoke *(effet de brouillard)*

However there is in Ashbery's poetry
a spontaneous figuration
leading to blind alleys and conduits

as with the map of *Gennevilliers* 1874
the dotted lines showing the location of new sewer outlets

here we enter a word-illusion where
meanings like scattered letters escape to find us

perhaps we are only confronted with the ephemeral
or constant interruptions to
our thought-patterns

interpretation claims more for the poem
than the poem needs to claim

On the bank of the river a bathing spot
appears overhung with trees.
From a different viewpoint

it is out of sight
a rubber fish swims by
a woman towards the left
margin shows evidence
of radical political intent
we wonder at this point
if there is a place
for us in the world
and if it's the place
we are in

The river is indigo
hard as iron and as
straight as a wall
it passes a large saw-mill
a chemical plant
a carbonated water factory
a cardboard-box factory
a rubber fish factory
and one making fine crystal

slightly downstream
from the highway bridge
there is singing
shouting
running about
falling over
and shagging

it all begins with
entrecôtes au cresson
and ends with
aching limbs

the day is full of mysteries
on a railway line out
of *Gare St Lazare*

Poem

Before I begin this poem
I would like to discuss the question of poetry itself

I can recall that in the ancient world
children learned poetry at school
it was ranked among the foremost of the liberal arts
it was forbidden to teach it to slaves

it was also held in renown by the Romans
Catullus always seemed to have his cock out
writing on the walls of temples
overlooking the sea

it's a fact that many useful skills
can be derived from poetry

a helpful tool for memory
for categorisation, patterning and decoration

the intricate knowledge it can provide
can be found in the fine details
of citadels, walk and subways,
rivers, canals and bridges (see over)
(air traffic control would seem to be in need
of some refinement)

indeed a reader
who does not esteem this kind of poetry
is obviously, politely, quite
wrong headed

Poem 2

today it is snowing in Naples
I will be there at 8
I suggest the girls go
to the top of the mountain
and jump off

they keep me awake at night
number 15A turned out to be pea-green
not the blood-red I imagined

it is not good taste to desire a dog
(I may well have misunderstood)

tomorrow I have a date in Tangiers
there the night has 1000 eyes
and in a week I will be in rue de Chaillot

I will look in on the Arab butcher
I told him it was published in 15 volumes
and cost 900 francs

my poems
26 Imaginary Landscapes
are to be in a little magazine

number 16A is
as grey as silver and coloured by blood
"what a horrible thing yellow is"

The Leisure Industry

outbreak of storms
                        oppressive heat from the city

Harvey Keitel in *Bad Lieutenant*
meets
is it *Madonna of the Harpies*
or *Madonna of the Baldachin*

July to August
if I were a Roman I'd stay in
my villa to oversee the grape harvest
life there more casual than in the cities
           I could spend my time
                chasing chickens, experiment with grafting trees
and rooting unusual specimens

blot out my past and the world's present

perhaps take a boat ride
          (the clogged Seine at Argenteuil)
or fish from a shore bench

and there upstream would be a little vine-covered pergola
providing a shady setting for a picnic

over the bridge would stroll an old man
such as owners of large estates will do with their guests
in the garden after a meal

pastimes include reading, gambling, particularly roulette
but the best games would be provided by *giochi d'acqua* –
the Jacuzzi
the water flow controlled by servants

respite from the heat would be found
inside an artificial grotto
like that of the Villa Giulia
or within a fountain house

all this of course is polite cultural capital, kudos and respect

it would be better to stay with Harvey and
tolerate the irritating annoyances and unbearable toils
of responsibility in the city

The Pictures

Paolo Uccello, Paolo di Dono more eccentric
her heart in silver filigree
describe her naked
describe him
that he makes good a metaphor
that there is much upkeep to the body
that you grow old
The King's beautiful daughter and her girdle
of stars, of a rich velvet, of plaited hair
of a string of semen
other versions of said such theme
that the cut is a real cut
that the lance penetrates the dragon and spouts
dog lites pop
guts pump
fields now bleached with waving rye
strings of pearls blob (translucent PVA)

this subject is very well known
death black planes

ii

the warrior on the white horse rides
so bravely into battle, the coral of his lisp, the flap of skin,
he has a mustard coloured orb, rubbing it twice nightly
LONELY INTERESTED IN STRANGE RESULTS
which seem to take place in a rose bordered orangery
the flames of candles spout
flowers, birds, oleander, nightingales
reading Yeats' poems as real estate problems
economies of war
riding into battle
PICTURES OF PRISTINA
postcard views *The Battle of San Romano*
the inventor of news (Theophratus)
the coral lagoon lipstick
her flesh flush
ROOM 4 with Botticelli *Tondo: The Adoration of the*

iii

Here is a poem by someone else
St Nicholas saves a ship from a storm by Matthew Barnes
A mermaid is swimming
134 Asniers is an industrial suburb of Paris
here a hymnic aspect is apparent
a fish is looking at another fish (from another poem)
the river is the Seine. Parts of the present are woven (bumps)
an orange hat BOY BY THE RIVER which he photocopied
address 707 Scott Street
3708 Utopia Parkway
something descends from the sky
lotus and raspberry
and now a conversation
lifts the ship out of the water
here further use of repetition and recombination
(I am grateful to my colleagues Mr Bulgina,
N.V. Pertsov and Mrs Rozencvejg for pointing out
these features) reshape novelty
and now one by me OVER THE STEPPES
and into a field
                        no trees but lots of mines

iv

the random and the orderly
dog and swing (park)
the European Room (being refurbished) Josip
Broz (in one work the planes are bees)
So dogfight and *S* wing (room)
Sonic boom and visual perception at once
LIVE WIRE DO NOT TOUCH
birds in random call on call through a lane of stitchwort
the refrain of the chaffinch
a cloud came over and then a plane
then a bird, here and here
singing through the ear
barked all night
Über den mühsamen aufgegangen
the blossoms of a dark earth

v

congruent walkways PALM FRONTED contusion
MELANCHOLY (see introduction and Chapter 10)
maybe on a distant shore
the names of boats, houses beach huts
the varnished glint on a slack sea
the ethics of tourism (prostitution, slavery)
LOOK THEY HAVE MIXED UP LANGUAGE TO NOTHING
to nothing, to nowhere, to no one
over the span of the sea
to nowhere and no one
perhaps a vase of
FLOWERS and BEES
the Floretines and the Sienese
this lively pageant
and the BEES ARE PLANES DIVING AND BOMBING
and the AIRCRAFT CARRIERS ARE HIVES
a city lit by flares
why are lemons boats
galoot and touch don't touch sticky to touch
DO NOT TOUCH
live
wire

vi

plan it X the future BOOM
cut to teeth of BABYLOTION FISH
sequested protesters at airport
BEES ARE PLANES ON JAUNTY FLIGHTS
narrow roads BEEP BEEP toot toot
rather good mini store, boys buy FANTA
orange BOOM flares
Look at me culture
and WINGED from a field blue flaxed
with roses bro
nzino VENUS with his arrow quiver
O the sweetness she brings may
be accompanied by pain
without connectives or subordination
"It's rosy garland on golden sands"

vii

the sound of rickshaws (stem association)
MOON-SOUNDER MOTH (Surinam)
break up rhythm
the long suckle SPUME GLIDER FISH (Moon Lake, Tennessee) with
crabs like MOON CRUSTACEANS
on carapace
fat lard cellulite or
HOW TO MAKE ARTIFICIAL SEA WATER (see page 68)
Never use pails
MOON WRASSE (Indo-Pacific)
got sucked in
Mr Frank de Graaf, a native Hollander
The NORTH SEA DOLIPHINARIUM
to ride a cock horse, MOONSHANKS
published by the Pet Library
Mono-fish (polyglot parrot) a kipper, lobster orange
occasional bits of liver (see anemone)
need booster dose for
may midnight melon moon
MOON WAILER
MOON BOMB

Paris

at last the chemist is open
the food you sent was wonderful
in the Art Shop the books were inexpensive
how can they afford to do it
but I didn't buy anything
I still have *Mysteries of Small Houses* and *The Book of Pleasures* to read
the doctor checks my pulse, "you'll need a whole new body soon" he says
I apply to replacement parts and the library of dreams
where my cyst grows larger every day
it's spring, nearly, the 29th Feb and there are daffodils in the garden
on the rue Rivoli there were small dogs and big turds
at the Cité metro a policeman lit a cigarette
I didn't see a flower anywhere
but I thought of James Schuyler's poems
the waitress near our hotel had beautiful hair
and I bought one of those diving angel postcards (Giotto)
sort of doodlebug over Florence
with some squint eyed saint looking up
golden beams shooting from his eyes
with a golden diskette behind his head
and I looked at them holding hands
thinking fuck where did all that time go
and we punched the code into the door and opened it
and up the stairs like the stairs in our apartment in rue Gabriel
and she said hello
and the memories came back
a collection of snow-shakers, eggcups
and Japanese seaweed

2

From *Europe* to *Père Lachaise*
Someone asleep right there on the pavement
10 Francs your cemetery guide
I don't look for long
I look at the news-stand
I'm thinking how and why did I get here
I'm thinking you've had it too, but the sun's in your eyes
And a little angel appears *Le songe de Joachim*
He's an androgynous blur, pink-winged with a golden CD diskette
I think Jim Morrison would be 57 now
I'm not impressed with their disregard for others
Their names scrawled over the dead
The Piaf grave covered in flowers
The Wilde grave by stencilled kisses
Alice asked if his penis was missing
Then the elegant Vietnamese graves
The graves of Jews and Arabs
A guard stands observing visitors to the Morrison grave
Scribbles, a candle, some wilted flowers and *I love you*
Doug tells me of the members of the Paris Commune
Who were executed and buried on the spot
Alice writes instructions for *Le Palet Lafayette* rue d'Hauteville
We have a coca-cola and a petit kronenbourg in a bar opposite a church
The evening traffic sweeps around an island
A flower shop is closing
A child rushes around the tables
It costs one Franc to piss
I have your book in front of me
I read the first poem

3

he had a little shop so I'm told
where he painted
just off Parc Monceau
Nude Men

later he met X
writing to him in detail of the great poet Y

and he'd start at night at the *Coronation of the Virgin*
or was it Hugo van der Goes
where in colour I can see the strings of puppets   and the
baby
has   boshed out   indenting the floor
it's got that grin on its face
but it hasn't got a diskette

the great poet Y said X found him irritating

and the canals of Bruges silted up

& he put on the kettle in his little shop
& all these nude men stood around in the steam
& he wrote *The Turkish Bath Lament*
he put a bustle in it
a torture table, a little dog (licking its parts)
some putti and some large ships

I think lots of them are jealous and envious of each other

Find The Black Sea

Find the Black Sea on a map and go East
It is a land of grassy hills
The grass is long and has many shades
That's where Anatol comes from
He had dreams of starting a computer dealership
Or a bee farm
He sits next to me
What am I interested in
I don't know enough for him and I never will
But I have the company of my friends
We live side by side
For years and years says Anatol
I wonder if his woman will marry him
I wonder if there will be babies
I will send my mother a clock
And my wife money for a television
I fear the army has found itself in a quagmire
Anatol writes poetry
He writes about the winds of our homeland
He says if he had a machine he'd record it
He says he can hear the bees making honey
He says he can feel the warmth of the wind in the wetness of the rain

At night he talks in his sleep of his mother
It is hot in our room even with the window open
I cannot believe they are the same stars
I think of the dates you gave me to remember
Birthdays and weddings
I think of the number of lights they have on their streets
Anatol's honey was the best
It was best with warm milk and cinnamon
When we were young we were happy
Here there is a park where I go sometimes

It has a museum
In the museum there are tiny carved wooden figures
I think they are slaves

Homer in Paris

Homer went to Paris 1867
Nebraska also 1867
listen to 59 in full colour, the prettiest sight
Glib Transom's cock going up in his trousers
(that's Maud Cook but that's 1895, Texas was 1845)
they tossed into the jetty with happy beaks,
strange signs and vaunted logos
I was in love that May or may
not, maybe November
a drained stillness on her face, hapless,
meanwhile we think we adopt democratic models,
hatless in the wind another day passes
traces of scarlet and crimson below the nail
California five years later
being thrilled therapeutically
big enough to get lost in
Bobbie was a boy in Morocco
licking her lips to be mine in the hut
holding starry lamps aloft, alight

Catskill on a locomotive

Catskill on a fast locomotive (later a train through Tarreytown)
on page four (actually 112 Landscape)
amplifies the scenery's primordalism,
in Cole's nature blasted trees perform various roles
Bobbie was Betti once with a wig
and then by coach in 1842
make yet what you will
it will be a great weekend in NYC
full of remorse and guilt
I am bound to fall through a darkened chasm

there's a tiny tourist well dressed
gesticulating at the heart of the poem
both amused and confused
maybe it has to do with the stupefying wilderness of words
or an interior spectator from another poem
(maybe Ireland 1862)

present in the chasm
vestiges of cloud patches,
forested mountains, well cultivated land and
10 spot the differences and I can't find one that matters
on the verge of inaugurating another
Betti was better than Bobbie any day

capital worries (the clean out)

speculations for profit

release all sperm

shell out

rub gecko grease in

float gemfish market

open ALL zoos

sprinkle and enjoy

Charlotte Apple

Apple Betti

roly poly

mal del pinto (disease of the spotted dick)

gematria

in the pipeline, see below

pinpoint, see under pin

to make or become pink

such as sea pink, Carolina pink, Grandma Pink, Indian pink, Johnny Humphead pink,

invisible pink

a beautiful blue

Indian ink

a blue winged humming bird

An Interlude

the fire is lit
Mrs Pink is at the stove
Johnny Humphead has made it out to sea
whilst she is cooking stovies in a radiant light
a sort of Membling blue suffuses
all and Mrs Pink comes over
all strange from a bird's eye point of view
maybe that midget angel in the top right
meanwhile Johnny's on his mobile
a stonking Virgin Mary colour
Mrs Pink stokes the fire
Johnny slicks his hair
die Wunde! die Wunde! cries Parsifal
Mrs Pink awaits his call
kitchen devil at hand
such are love's wounds
perhaps she will use ring back
perhaps she will compose a stornello
in order to dance the dance of love

One's Confusion With The East
(with Bob Cobbing)

Sometimes in Zendo I can hear my refrigerator
I can hear my neighbour putting a lot in
It is not easy to make sense out of its purring
I can hear the rain falling into frogs spawn
I can feel dogs dancing on the lawn
It's not easy to make sense out of lines like that
And then we get lost in what they may imply

We chant dharanis which can only be vaguely translated
You chant the way you groan in pain
I can hear the rain falling into frogs spawn
I can hear my neighbour putting in a lot of joy
It's not easy to make sense out of lines like that
When each word contains not itself but more
And meaning soaks into the soil like rain

Sometimes in Zendo I can hear the rain dancing in joy
We chant like frogs these wet spring days
I can hear you wondering if I am shouting in pain
I am thinking what is in the refrigerator?
I sit up straight and breathe one syllable at a time
Without hindrance, there is no fear
The frogs jump in joy and splash through puddles*

*that is their way

A History of Hydraulics

They went out with baskets looking for truffles
Oh these musical painters from Prague
a nova rich sky of astral and beam
and set themselves down on junkets to browse
and sunbolt bright a sign appeared
with the impact of water on water
veemenzia, furiositá, impetuositá, concorso

Oh these musical painters from Prague
with their little letter word magnet collections
fridge ducks, phonetic trees and *loaves of love,*
a nova rich sky above their slaphappy heads
over a weir the impact of water on water
catching with a bright plastic bucket the words
veemenzia, furiositá, impetuositá, concorso

And they were jollied out like stockbrokers on
the tongues of pigs and calves in sausage skin
Oh these musical painters from Prague
their notebooks filled with infinite combinations of
letters and indeed in Fig 111
a fishing boat is a word magnet catching the words
veemenzia, furiositá, impetuositá, concorso

First Anti Poem

A terrified knight flees a giant green snail
Sir John of Kidwelly was in Flanders
much like a three day long weekend in Amsterdam
smoke dope and get fucked
for the marriage of Margaret
1468 I think

At this time I feel we are doomed
the world filled with vanity and violence
ruled by lions and dragons

in the Ural distance the lion is one of the three beasts
watching the distant sun
shine on the shrine of St Ursula
(which is a hospital in Bruges)

this all might seem unnatural for a poem
it seems unnatural for life!
yet everything the poet fakes is real

note that interpretation consists
of an abyssal spiral of ironies,
words are always likely to be problematic and unpredictable

the dark wood where the straight way is lost

William of Ockham based his philosophy, *nominalism*
On visual experience
     If I say what I have seen who will believe me

how could Sir John's report of Amsterdam contain a sheep, a horse
               and a cat,

at the head of the page lies a flight-type and a flock-pattern
other pages contain shellfish and insects drawn close up yet seen from
                                                                      a distance

the text omits but the margins include

indeed the invention of eyeglasses must have helped
just think of all those problems monks must have had with writing
                                                                       technology,
Cardinal Nicholas of Rouen peers at this text as though looking at
minute marginal detail
what is he looking at
it is not a map of *naturalness*
or the constants in our changing natures
but a map of Europe between 1351-52

XXXXXXXXXXXXXXXX

the grisaille shows a flat disc from the Urals
Ipse dixit et facta sunt
somewhere over the rainbow
and I do set my bow in the cloud
and I watched *The Fourth Protocol* (Feb 18 00)
corruption again at the highest level
and it came to pass in the days of
vegetarianism that animals had no fear of man
and I played the disc late at night
setting free the gigantic birds Zipper and Treat
and in the five hundredth year of the second millennium
men caught fire having intercourse with each other, the beasts and
                                                                    women
and I sat down with my diskette and grisgris
to write *A History With Naked People (sicut erat in diebus Noe)*

The Next Poem

defeated by (I don't know what and everything)
I stem a flow
I've stopped now but the words wobble out in some form
They are the last Mars probe
They are proboscis explorer

They are the road to insouciance
A world gone pot-noodle

I have tried cotton wood
Bristol tarts and armour paste

Whack it hard

The tongue lollops by a frontispiece
How long can I hold on to a dying breath,
                          a moon slick or a daisy pearl

I have brushed remonstrance from my crown
I have entered the bad days
I have written clever clogs (but he hasn't answered)

Those old questions

In my own way I have tried to improve both body and mind
I have rubbed cream and breathed powders
I have showered in heaven's gel
Poured oyster and pomegranate dust

Only the other night I ran off to the woods
Where the moon shaved a path with Jan van Eyck light

There were golden shards in its tracings
And that which should have appeared more shaded was brighter

Woods are invariably frightening
A broken path bemoans us, is there a right road?
No longer geometric (unlike the line of the bazaar, see earlier work)
The path turns spiral, then rectilinear it
Spits and forks away to

Some place where there isn't any trouble

D'you suppose there is such a place, Toto?

The Artist's Life

we have the distribution of light and shade
of meaning and unmeaning

in plate XXI he has his knackers out
with little insect wings attached
in the bottom left she dispatches the Winged Monkeys
it is a Jitterbug
Dr Jughead appears

and I looked up and said I am in the dark and I am

here the presence of reflection informs us perhaps
of what St Augustine was thinking

Toto is heading for a piss by the tumtum trees
to his left in plate XXII a lion fucks with a wolfgirl

Figs 1 and 2 show St Augustine with a hurricane lamp
walking through cloisters on what looks like a wet March windy day
Goethe describes this as *die Taten und Leiden des Lichts*
(the actions and suffering of light)
the sheer bulk of his thinking
            testifies to the doubts preoccupying his mind,
the pinched, shrivelled expression I put down to corns or bunions

It was here she said to him
take off your garments and mine
the morning plumed her golden breast
toto caelo
temptress verbatim
a sort of *visum effuientes**

in this way Gen Pinochet is said to be brain damaged

well what light do the wicked see in themselves?

*escaping the eye

This poem is concerned with the presentation
and documentation of natural processes and systems.
Such as feeding birds, balloons escaping into the air,
the slow release of words (initially) from the pen,
whirlpools and maelstroms
                                      This stanza contains the idea of a
                                            weather system as
you breathe taking my young in your mouth or a zen
garden as seeds dispersed by ejection, birds
consuming wild cherries, the cherry itself being
both bitter and toxic.
                       Some poems make little progress, due to
                                                error linkage,
the suggestion that hand gestures led to writing, the goodbye
of the chain leading to the handle of the cistern, the rattle of
the rails connecting one face to another. Time and again a
perfect mismatch.

This Poem

this poem is not copied from nature
but copied like the text from an earlier example
it does have what it does and doesn't contain
it doesn't discuss orthography, though would like to
and names are misspelled on both sides of the word

opposite is a rock and because it is a rock it is also a world
the world is not copied from nature
but copied in the colours of the rocks contained by it
the poem is not concluded when finished
which is known and unknown
which in the balance is not a question
the rock is lapis lazuli
it cools internal heat when powered and mixed with milk
it can cure fevers and blindness
(how we drift apart the poem and the copier)
nature is after all inherently magical
take the garden, which cannot be copied from nature,
is it not an aesthetic and economic convention,
and what happens in the Roman de la Rose?
The poem, basically an internal space, is exploited not for itself
but what it contains, like the garden of the poem, which
is not nature, is economic being copied into a text
from an earlier example

                                        figures hang outside
which could transform the interior spaces into sunny simulacra
the garden is loaded with meaning
if that is what the copier intends
then the natural world is too wild, which seems fitting enough,
to be included.

1.   The poet intended to write a poem of a tree.
She had a tree in front of her (out of the window
in a small pot a bonsai on the table). An actual tree
therefore features in the poem and initiates the cause
of the poem's appearance, whether or not the poem
in fact resembles a tree. The poet calls the poem *Tree*

2.   The poet did not intend to write a poem about a tree.
She did not have a poem in front of her as she was writing.
No tree was written in the writing of the poem. However when
the poem was finished it reminded the poet of Japan
and she called it *Tree* for that reason.

3.   The poet left the poem without a title. When it was
published certain readers thought the poem reminded them
of a tree and not Japan although the poet included neither
a tree nor Japan in her poem. The poem has though looked
like a tree since the poet finished writing the poem.

Temptress: A Timeless Theme

I now no longer know who
writes these, neither who they are intended for,
if I have intention

arguments surround tastes,
especially in poetry, I
counsel patience, work at it,
for pleasures are perhaps to be gained,
hopefully

I don't know how the words were originally
grouped or
in what sequence, yet
they are only a part of the plethora of accessible images
some of wax
some of wood
available to the plumber,
some of iron
for the deep throated
and some of salt-sapphire
however they may well all be hedonistic

if you are to take up this art
my advice would be to
learn new words
not to write in obscurities,
give a line plinth hair or
a wood nymph
attach phrases in plenitude
there is scope for innumerable combinations
keep a check on
the mathematical architecture
the weight and balance of lines

in this way a lobe can tickle a bum
on the buttock or better a wood nymph's breasts
hot-tempered she may be
but you can have
a hand raising a blessing

and yet the prevailing mood
of tranquil harmony
is deceptive
rude words have been removed
(see *The Stone Operation*, the surgeon
wearing a funnel shaped hat),
it would make me sit bolt upright
revealing me to be full of
plastic tubes, guttering and conceit

these gatherings of daily distraction
can be tidied away,
votive offerings whitewashed
(police and government tactics)
polyptychs rejected to sacristies

words can only thinly reproduce
a sense of objects
yet trivia and profundity
can mingle

in the end (ah Saints)
there are no depoliticised views
to oaks in general, to forests,
the inclosure of them,
waste lands, crown lands
and government

and when I arrive
will she be there to greet me
running through the leaves
bare vellum in her hands

Temptress Two

The reader can rest assured that
the eggplants grow in a poisoned soil
and the flowers will wilt before evening.
I gaze across a landscape of letters and trees
or are the trees letters
or the letters trees – everything is in blossom
whilst the sun persists in illuminating crude titles.
Modernity is not being overlooked
neither is a bright bucolic handling of breasts.
There are scraps of Egyptian linen
on the fence within a criss-cross of lines and figures
written in grass and waves
or waves of grass.
Are the lumpish boys bathing
and in what kind of water
where more than 120,000 cubic litres of solids
have accumulated.
Maybe after all I do not have any clear ideas
about landscape or poetry
where lives look like lies
alas they're only words in letters
or letters in words
but I believe the main element of my speculation
to be the countryside organised to attend
the pleasures of the middle class

Temptress Thee

Look life isn't like that
examples are obvious
the man, for instance, is ostensibly floating
(opaque blob in the water)
seemingly to belong to a pool of people,
we fool ourselves.

The other is across the river in front of the house
given away by the unlikely angle
of a straw hat
its general lack of fit
tilted forward as if hiding behind
a real piece of machinery,
the bluntness of the blue against yellow
creates a dissonance of colour
from a harmony of intention.

This river has fashioned a debris
of bits and bobs
of carotage
of muddied limbs and heads.

And across towards Mersea
where we'll eat
the Romans ate well on oysters
Pliny the Younger wrote to Tacitus about Vesuvius
on a river of indigo
towards a trollop
he was just about to shag

Temptress Three

I remember snow
the town constantly changing shape
not just at the edge of the poem

wide tools were built to shift it
drains laid for the thaw

it was 1875 before the town was painted
and it spite of the snow
it gave way to steam, a marsh and a few trees
leading to a railway station

                      now snow is falling
                a dilute sun struggling through oily clouds
                people holding umbrellas

Camille is stiff jointed on a bench
a broken toy on the whitened grass
a washed-out silence
and the trees in winter look like letters bare of leaves
they speak in waves
a great din of emptiness

                doe tracks
                birds pecks
                laid for lunch

a melting, watery stillness
and the wife
the husband
looking the opposite way
sun wax upon cold blue and white
a finely woven tablecloth

Tempted

I knew nothing of Baudelaire
but I had read his name on a wanted poster
or was that Apollinaire

those calligrams of bird droppings
I imagine over spring fields
with fumble on his mind
in someone's undergarments
pegged out on a line

Let me tell you I had such a surprise
when I wrote to Baudelaire
that which turned out to be
a poem without tress
or was it a painting without letters
a smile glowing upon my face

O I am so silly
my right lobe not knowing what the left is doing
pegging out letter *A's,* writing little umbrellas,
performing charitable acts
scratching my name on trees

love has me on the edge of
such excellent times

he has shown me sketches of his testicles

I keep them next to my heart

and a tattoo on his buttock

he keeps his in his pocket
warmed by his right hand
as he walks the Boulevard de Clichy
or crosses Le Pont de l'Europe

what could I return to him
but a poem for this new century

a threesome possibly on a bed
or sprawled full length upon the summer grass
in some shade perhaps
a place of awkward angles
holding his stick
keeping his hat on
I wish I could write in French
and understand metrics
before I attempt another

Tosso the Great

Apparently the King of Naples was a fine poet
a prize winner and Olympic medallist—of course
he was an amateur
and not a professional
gifted from an early age
he wrote in many forms

columns, squiggles, hieroglyphs and ideogrammic combinations
but sound poetry was beyond him
in some rift valley
or alpine hut

He wrote a treatise on poetry
unfortunately or not
now lost

II

Tosso made a careful study of Euclid
in order to write mathematically constructed lines
but also to understand the writing of others

meanwhile his friend Fabio
took up football with Lazio
in place of poetry
realising he was not a man of letters

"my concerns are better handled through football
than bookishness"

nevertheless he wrote 116 books of poetry
which indeed is a useful indicator of
his wide range of interests
and his growing linguistic competence

in his library
besides 7 religious texts
he had
a Dante
a copy of Josephus
Ovid and Petrarch
books by Ted Berrigan, Tom Raworth, Geoffrey Hill
Lisa Robertson, Bob Cobbing, Bern Porter and Sean O'Brien

Tosso developed the three dimensional poem
these *pattern* poems were principally
concerned with animals, birds and plants

many of the animals were re-used in later poems
the lion for instance

his friend Lorenzo asked him
if he might have back the sheets of birds
he had lent to him

Tosso made a small model artist's book
containing visuals and language motifs
these poems included references to rejected
notions of narrative composition
his young wife Sibyl and

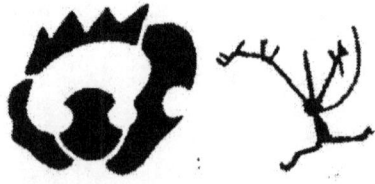

some sylphs around a hot mud-pool
based on Antonio Pollaiuolo's *Battle of the Nudes*

III

I would like to sing in a travelling choir
to play the *lira da braccio*
to perform honest acts,
      working as a diplomat or spy
I would write dummy poems
made of unfamiliar words with obscure meanings

my reward to be a parcel of land
or perhaps a terracotta plaque
hanging in the garden signifying
Winter with
an inscription by Ian Hamilton Finlay

and on the reverse a tank
and some Latin

through singing I would make visible
rain, cloudy mountains and villages,
the stars above us, rays, mists
and the love-light
in a person's eyes

IV

I now have the details of 5 poems I wrote in a dream

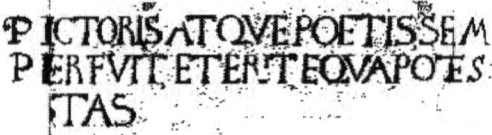

men of uncommon beauty emerging from the bath
one whose face and breast is clearly seen
but whose hind parts are in a mirror written
on the page opposite so that you may read his back as well
as his front enfolding colour cadences
where the sun shines on the image of a bee
a cryptic choreography

betrothal
brothel,
a sprig of eryngium in his hand

further, perhaps painted on a wall a landscape filled with *amorini*
the sea and foam are real
and the wind seems to blow with gold highlights
over a dulled skyline

but these are clear signs of agitation
a tempest at sea, thunder and lightning
a city in conflagration
under torsion and stress

and in the mirror looked at in a previous poem
I could see entirely the other side
his feet at the edge of a clear and limpid brook
a saint's plate over his head
the city about to fall
filled with the reflections of light from metal

the random shapes clouds take up
and *fantasia*

Part One Puškin

I have been with myself day & night
through unnumbered forest
until I knew the flowers by touch and name
leading to the border where words elude reason
I have seen them in hyphens stitching parts
white lining the way for dogs
to the flame of the shrine on the olive road
to the gnarled tree where
the Dragon-bird broods over his eggs
hatching pharmacies of pain
give me the fourth syllable so I may relax between your caesura
look this is a beautiful poem
& how he hated Heine for it
strange to read it in Russian with the phonological
rook pasting his beak to *A* for apple
hammering the jelly-worm of words to the wall
nailed there root and branch
and running into nothing but a juice stain

Schelling describes him as *unhinged*
there is a split spruce *(v)* in the forest of dichotomies
the resin trails in splatters from the wound
I've tried not to be ill
but you're there with your succubus
at the shelf of "smellies" (Where are you tonight _____?)
                                                                   (fill in the blank)
you've powdered over your hyphen-trail with snow
till it whiffs with the aromas of shop peach and stale avocado
disguising that scarred after effect of the detonated image
it's no good leaving those pebbles as signs
they look like isolated snow-berries
I have studied the relations of explicitness and ambiguity,
there, I want to be your pot-bellied pregnancy,
I want your unguents over my eyes
I want to write wee people are a dialogue
I want to stitch the wound's chagrin
I want to go to work in the morning & forget about it all
the cold frost gathering on the grating

I can take the sky's hatch off
a door which has become *unhinged*
(I'll replace it with stitching)
shapes fill the air
birds like flat black pieces of cloth
and in the corner the Dragon-man writes
the infinity of isolated moments
he has written in embryo searching for the monologic
the ink is red-russet bearing the heat of the hearer's attention
or bits of paper (confetti) rice for the rook to pick at
such a syndrome strikes me
that the buildings are jelloid full of grammatical shifters
there are goats grazing for meaning
the field is a slop of oil green
the conga will peck at it with numb teeth
turning it into chains of *abstracta*
I will work the needle burned in a flame
to sear the wound

all this yearning & you want nothing from me
you go to the anteroom & play your greatest hits
these are only fine grains of silica
the shape-bird like a folded *v* flops at your part
a sequence of atoms as it were
dropping the *n* into a somersault
having verbal intercourse with his partner
striking at the last tiger pelt with a hacksaw
your eyes aglow with the abandonment of deixis
& you don't starve for me in some advent pine
& you don't listen to the song of the singing leaves
& you don't hear my tremulous cringe
& there's little you would write down
until you've erased my name from the paper
you took the roots first until I became balloon headed
a nocturnal sound made from dense wood
planting me in a field of aphasia
& handing me to seekers of curiosities

morning, and the bird skews across the light
morning, and you whistle for your dog
morning, and the day is placed by catchment
the sink shines with a hint of lemon
morning, where the frost has gathered on the grating
there is a glow in the distance
in the yard your shoulder is framed by the window
fresh butter-light catches your hair
morning, later you'll brush away the fallen leaves
read it in the paper's rote of despair & disaster
read it in the shower of getting *b* from *a*
read it in the lines written on your palm
hear it in the lexis which falls rainbow sweet from your tongue
hear it in the warming day as a garden bee
hear it as I wrap my shirt over my fence
hear it as my teeth bite echoes into my toast
I kiss his cheek and hold him as I go
breaking down into sentiment & mannerisms

look there's that rook at your apple again
(they bunch in flagging knots, unloose & unravel)
was he talking writing to himself
trying to disassociate himself from bargain buys,
no words better that some
because the fields open with buttercups or silica
& you put *this* to *that*
as hat to head, heart to mouth,
note the paronomasia & dactylic meter
the rooks tip to the mountainside,
they fly and stray & together
upfold & adjust in strata
they've done their *cawing* like the stream's _____
                              (fill in the blank, again)

pausing here & there to take breath
I take up your deceit & call it lying

morning again, the thrush in the falling
fruit and leaf of pear tree
was all that nightmare, & the gift of sleep
the Moon-man ceased,
he is pear shaped & holds a moon-lion in his hands
his hands melt moon-ice tears
in the folds of broken leaves
the thrush shuffles her beak for respite
the October sun sparkles ice-like off the grass
& there the melon slice of moon full of star-seeds
the sun throbs in my head
a line of Puškin fills it
in an incomprehensible language
I feel the line of rough stitches with butterfly grip
maybe the blackest coffee will straighten me out
or the noise of my children stumbling down the stairs

afternoon & I'm beginning to wane
the light is being stripped from the sky
the occlusions gather over the keepsake album
I'll remember you there in the midst of those masculine lines
they weren't dull times, were they?
how can I hear the noise of a wave splashed against my head
how can I hear your thick arm through the air
unstitching my living hem with the bird's breast,
ah you have it, we are mutually contradictive
what is there for you in my name
do you think the fish feels like this raised from the water
why am I snapping the pages shut
why is the bird's beak like a razor with red
please put the fish back
put the blue back in the sky
paint the waxed sun grease once more all over my dry lips

Puškin Part Two

now I have dissected the syntax behind you
here in the Ukrainian forest
black birds beat under the breast
the meaningless alternation of wave upon Dave,
Puškin has a ladder in his tights, that's
Dave Puškin, he cannot go to the bowl in the wood
                the trees are dark where the dead birds hang
fake fat wood pigeons for the hunting lobby,
decoys, the trees tufted, sprinkled with
cocaine icing sugar, desiccated coconut.
Mr A. de Groot wears galoshes
we discuss Mr A. V. Isacenko's case theories as we chat along
we have dedicated grease and rice papers to his form
some real life is a bowl of soup
some real life is not some bowl of soup
a wave that has splashed against some distant shore
until your life is washed clean and empty on the draining board

it will die like that sad noise
it is spilled over the world's edge,
daylight, the squeezed breakfast orange,
black through the strainer of oak and beech
last rattle of the late train
where the boats go,
the name will be heard no more
it will vanish without a trace, will die
my name in silence,
the world's brim
look here are the contiguities of tense and number
of vernal aspect and choice
why can't I slaver over my thoughts
a mixture of barley and oats, of verbal aspect and voice
why is there a forest before the window of cloth
it reduces the vantage to nil
I will return by the first quatrain
it's tin like rattle and life's little spark

love has dried out
the sea's splash against my cheek,
some washed-up distant shore
will leave a dead trace akin
to our combining
the morphological shift of synthetic fabric and skin
juiced out in twilight
waxed and gone
why didn't I cotton on to
the fatal limitedness of all action,
on the line of whitened snow I uttered
the frozen expression *daj vam Bog*
all I can recall are clean sheets,
new clean sheets and the sun of that landscape
surrounded by too much and not enough
both vernal and verbal
both wave and Dave
splish, splash and splosh

last year you planted an artichoke
the world has changed so much you yearn
spent spit and elbow grease on polishing
getting to the heart of the worktop
like nocturnal shapes in dense woods
there was an inlaid line we had to follow
Mr Isacenko tempted us with fats
until it shone polyurethanely bright, clear silk or satin
it bears your reflection
and the garden the pansies that flourish there
it still bears fruit
the stuffed artichoke hearts glisten in coated oil
but on a day of sadness, in silence
there is no one to carry you off
now April's here like a Soutine somewhere in Sussex
in some far off place Helen you take on the name Dave
it ripples down my spine
there are ripples down my spine
there is in the world a knothole heart in which I live

now as I reach this hour
the sun settles the last of long shadows
you are cast to me in all this darkness
say *ture* like the *ture* in picture where the sun shines
it shines at the end of the bowered wood
into a May meadow
but on a day of sadness, in silence
here I flounder
as you drove home, half there, perfume
filling the car,
a pale yellow mustard daubed over a sea
the interior warmth between us expended along
a coast line of fading energy
straining towards an impetuous future
avidly leaving the past behind
I stumble besides Mr Isacenko into the Ukrainian forest
thick with fallen leaves

here he has painted his words
although abstract it looks like a gloomy forest
and into this dark wood we enter
laying the foundations for a new theory
conjoining pretty far fetched ideas
in new and stormy agitations
listen the sun has shed its first rays
they splash on the Volga
I count up the error of my ways on one hand (shh)
have I been bad
do I exaggerate
what do others think of me
there is no obligatory parallelism of markedness
the guilty do not speak
at least I have lived a life in the open air
thick with autumn's leaves

gear shifts in dense woods
knotholes, chairs, settees, beds all frottage in memory
the click-clack of a wooden shoe
so much so that locational meanings are so much sonar
displayed as paw prints,
phylacteries of piss marks, fruit stains bitter bright
I'm gathering partial word families like lost sheep in
the heart of the Ukrainian forest
sonorous in *flow, flutter, flirt*
Xlebnikov lets fly a gold script of veins
the stars are the fish swimming in the heavenly ocean
they dimple the snow of the sky in a frozen lake
the air is full of strange pulsations
there is nuance after nuance in wood shavings
I become dislodged disengaged dispirited
a mountain goat as white as white hanging on an incline
I count my blessings
sun tomorrow, minus 51 celsius and
the faint sounds of falling snow

The Littoral Zone

I

all these shells man can easily observe
what he cannot see lies beneath his feet
an *I-beam* away is all it seems
but modern life calls for refits and centrefolds
tightening our belts makes things ***bulp***
stresses as you well know can be
tensional, compressional or torsional
now in this late hour almost at twilight
the shells on the beach glitter
and the plumes in the mantle flare

II

being carried away we move into deeper water
will the planet shrink?
I think of a collation of fruits
the top most layer banana seaweed
your skin the colour of *Frosties*
snowflakes detaching from both sides where
never mind we are all putty in the jaws of vice
ocean floors can be found in mountain chains
I think the squeeze is on

III

why do things break up
Pangaea broke up some 2200 *m.y.* ago
hospitals are full of suture zones
there are damaged lagoons with corrupted corals
Hades is full of America with high turbidity levels
there are no replacement parts to death
but we are struck dumb
talking in shopping menus
it seems as though there are simple linear plots
soft dimples in the air
and quality sponges in the rocky sublittoral

IV

winds generate shear stress
as the earth moves a tidal wave surrounds it
animals in the reducing zone have to employ anaerobic processes
I have a designer kit
so that the words silt and pebble
can be measured in microns
and not once have we mentioned porosity
your hair grey drizzle
and your eyes sharp pebbles
the days silt
in the water which engulfs us

V

what was important
is now not a question
there are long narrow troughs in poetic hot air balloons
the Earth's surface moves independently of its interior
you have your head in a book
and there is much displacement
that sinking feeling
how do we survive in this low velocity zone
watching redshank walk over mirrored mud
evidently in life there is a great need for prediction
on both local and global scales

VI

the white abalone is now an endangered species
did you live in Bolivia
was Olive Oil discovered there
16 men on a dead man's vest
and the sediment which underlies all
when it lithifies forms bands of chert
the way anchovies are packed into tins rather than jars?
and yet all in the end form nekton
sardines heated on toast
and the spawning manta ray and the kingclip

Uruk

All of a sudden nothing is there
In seas, on trees and animals
Falling sun-stones
Mirabalia of blood, flesh, milk and iron
Ineffable balls of noise
The invasion of guns
Infectious sweating sickness
A fine ash
In the air and in the heavens
Care nothing for it
There was a breeze all the time
The face of, the voice of
Who hacks men down
In Uruk saying to his mother

I shall now inform you of another
Seen by myself
coming from my Living
A little before 8 o'Clock in the Evening
to see a long Stream of
molten glass
Which shot down
a fine lambent Flame
meteoro-fanos
And continued
Parallel to the horizon
Until it changed into this
And into this
Other form
There was a breeze all the time
The Phenomenon was in place
In the city of Ur

There was a gentle Breeze all the time
Which shot down from A to B
I guess about 20 degrees
A long stream of like golden piss
Of acceleration and rupture
Muddy snow-water in a lucid pink sky
There *Nebuchadnezzar* carved in the brick
Six days and seven nights
In the air and heavens
The wind blew the downpour of
Water, stones, metals
And the lakes flared until
The pale star burst
Grew fainter and fainter
To a fine lambent flame
Till it vanished intirely about 9 o'clock

And the dogs made assault
Meeting them on the other side of the river
Some of them with their teeth
Frozen water on their backs
Pale star-burst of dust sprinkled auguries
Like snow their dying days
A fine ash
From the rising of to the setting sun
Slowness and viscosity of the blood
Parallel to the Horizon
Paraffin fires flared
Sea-birds in slicks of it
By stealth, wickedness and lie
A touch of wild imagining

Quickly alive and quickly gone
Taken from us
Looking to the clouds *ta meteora*
A fireburst she's said to have seen
Fiery rods, a Serpent, a Pyramid and a toothbrush
A touch of wild imagining (*meteor-geomes*) no doubt
Bestowing on us some hope
Of purging venom
To be as strong as a rock from the sky
Up the sacrificial stairs
Try purchasing peace
From falling sun stones

We are in a skiff in the sky
Out on the rim of the earth
Where paraffin flames fire
Cropping up where the eye rests
I am taken aback to how much little sense there is
Or what I can make of it
I would radio for help
Pale star burst of hope
A happiness I want for
Collecting camel dung for fire
Or settling to some sweetmeat but it is
As though there were two suns in the sky
As though the earth were riven
Exposing her folds
Illustrating a perspective of loss
Ever far off a meteor portents the hours

www.ingramcontent.com/pod-product-compliance
Lightning Source LLC
Chambersburg PA
CBHW032056150426
43194CB00006B/551